ME and my CAT

written by
Michael Dahl

art by
Zoe Persico

Curious Fox
a capstone company-publishers for children

First published in 2016 by Curious Fox,
an imprint of Capstone Global Library Limited,
264 Banbury Road, Oxford, OX2 7DY
Registered company number: 6695582

www.curious-fox.com

Printed and bound in China.

ISBN: 978-1-78202-522-1
20 19 18 17 16
10 9 8 7 6 5 4 3 2 1

A CIP catalogue for this book is available from the
British Library.

This is me . . .

. . . and my cat.

My cat and I like having fun. But cats can be picky about fun.

We like running and jumping
and lying in the sun.

I like swimming and diving, too. But my cat does NOT like the water.

My cat and I like
climbing up high.

I like hanging upside down,
but my cat does not.

I like when my mum
gives me a BIG hug.

My cat doesn't like big hugs
or being petted too much . . .

Puuurrr . . .

. . . unless it's on HER terms!

My friends and I like to play
and chase each other.

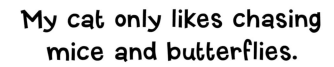

My cat only likes chasing
mice and butterflies.

Cats have their own way
of having fun, but we
always like being together.

A NOTE FROM CAT

Hi friend,

    I like you and hope we can be friends forever. Here are a few things to remember to keep our friendship going:

- **BE KIND**: Pet your cat softly.
- **BE CONSIDERATE**: Do not chase or sneak up on your cat.
- **BE POLITE**: Let a sleeping cat sleep and an eating cat eat.
- **BE CALM**: Do not steal your cat's toys or play rough.
- **BE GENTLE**: Never hit, pull, poke, ride or tease your cat.
- **BE RESPECTFUL**: Respect your cat's space.

    Above all, treat your cat how you want to be treated. Your cat will be the best friend it can be if you're a good friend too!

Yours,

Cat